Commissioned by the Midland Michigan Music Teachers Association for its Ke

The Grand Finale

primo

Proud and uplifting, with great energy and vitality ($\quad$ = 116–120)

* The pedal will sustain the right hand in ms. 30–32 so that it can be lifted, allowing the left hand to play.

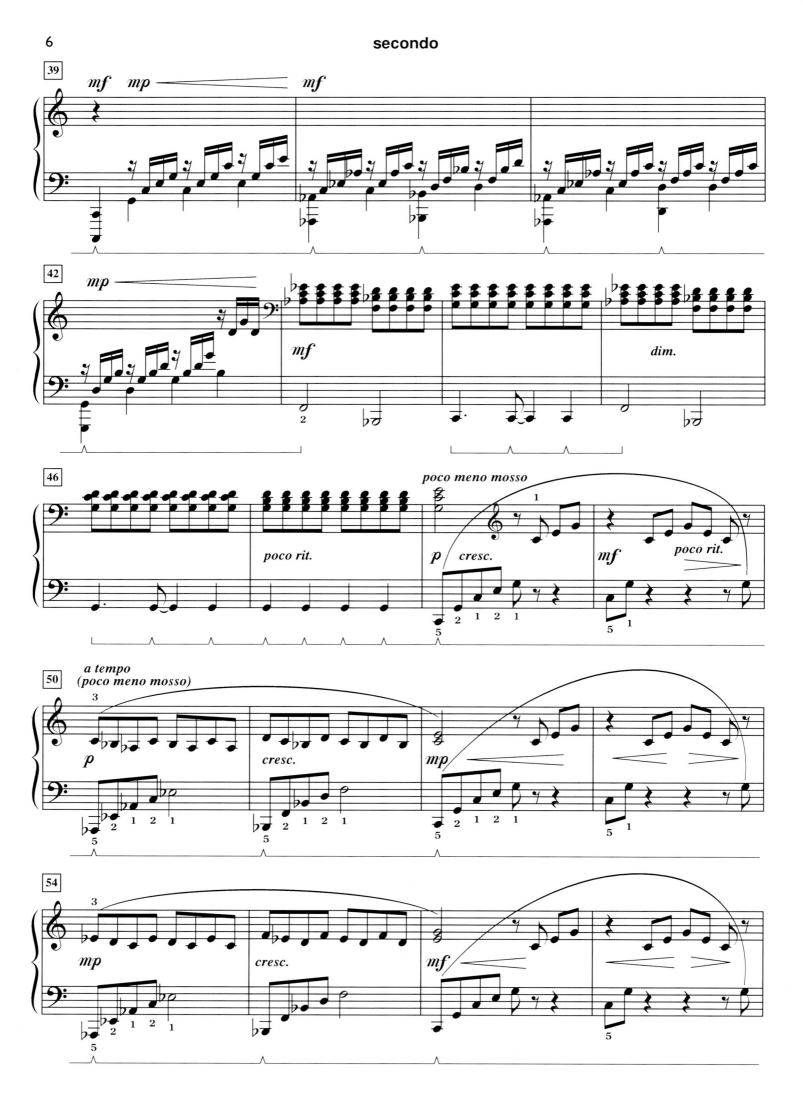

secondo

primo

a tempo, slightly broader

Favorite Duets from Alfred

Classics for Piano Duet *(Tingley)*

Offer beginners the opportunity to play the classics. By dividing the pieces between two performers, the parts are simpler but the overall effect is rich and sparkling.

Dances for Two *(Rollin)*

These duets capture the essence of dance music. Both the primo and secondo parts are written at the same ability level. Book 1 includes a French waltz, a jig, a tap dance, and a baroque dance. Book 2 includes a Charleston, a polka, a Russian waltz and a rock and roll dance.

Duet Classics for Piano *(Kowalchyk/Lancaster)*

These unique volumes contain duets in their original form written by composers who lived in the 18th, 19th and 20th centuries. The primo and secondo parts are written on facing pages and are of equal difficulty.

Duets for Animal Lovers *(Goldston)*

These indispensible collections add variety and help make practicing the piano become less work and more fun! The primo and secondo parts are equal in difficulty and the hand positions are shown for each piece.

Easy Classical Piano Duets
for Teacher and Student *(Kowalchyk/Lancaster)*

A valuable assortment of teacher/student duets in their original form written by teachers and composers during the 18th and 19th centuries. The student parts are limited to 5-finger position and fall primarily within the grand staff reading range.

Essential Keyboard Duets *(Kowalchyk/Lancaster)*

Book 1 includes 40 duets by Brahms, Mozart, Schubert, Stravinsky and more. Book 2 contains 25 waltzes, gavottes, marches and dances from around the world. The French repertoire in Book 3 includes Fauré's "Dolly Suite," Debussy's "Petite Suite," Ravel's "Mother Goose Suite," as well as 5 pieces from Bizet's "Jeux d'enfants." Essential ornamentation is realized in footnotes, both parts contain measure numbers and brief composer biographies are included.

First Favorite Duets *(Olson)*

Easy 5-finger arrangements of the world's most popular melodies, designed to encourage independent reading. Duet accompaniments provide a fuller sound.

Five-Star Classical Duets *(Alexander)*

Students will have fun exploring classical, operatic, orchestral and piano music through these arrangements of works by Bach, Mozart, Beethoven, Verdi and Liszt. Both primo and secondo feature the melody and are equal in difficulty.

Five-Star Folk Duets *(Alexander)*

These colorful arrangements make it possible for elementary pianists to experience the joy of duet playing at the earliest opportunity. Each player gets a chance to play the melody and lyrics are included for every selection.

Folk Song Portraits *(Alexander)*

Charming duet arrangements perfect for spicing up recitals and as supplementary material for group piano instruction in colleges and universities.

Jazz, Rags & Blues for Two *(Mier)*

The magic of Martha Mier's *Jazz, Rags & Blues* is back in this series—*Jazz, Rags & Blues for Two*. Enjoy the syncopated rhythms, colorful sounds and rich harmonies of jazz in a variety of styles.

Just for You & Me *(Alexander)*

Syncopation, singing melodies, tender ballads, mixed meters and mellow contemporary sounds are all found in this collection, designed to provide hours of musical enjoyment.

Kaleidoscope Duets *(George)*

These books introduce the student to a wide variety of musical designs and colors that spark the imagination while developing technical skills.

Music for Sharing *(Goldston)*

The wide variety of styles presented in these 3 books are perfect for recitals, sight-reading or just for fun! Some primo parts can also be played on their own as solos.

Terrific Tunes for Two *(Mier)*

The duets in *Terrific Tunes for Two* will encourage students to play with imagination. Both the primo and secondo parts are written at an equal level of difficulty.

Treasures for Two *(Mier)*

These two volumes each contain 6 captivating duets in various styles including blues, jazz, ragtime and even a tango! Both the primo and secondo parts are written at the same level of difficulty.

Alfred Alfred Publishing Co., Inc.
16320 Roscoe Blvd., Suite 100
P.O. Box 10003
Van Nuys, CA 91410-0003
alfred.com

ISBN 0-7390-130
GRAND FINALE

P8-BAV-496

9 780739 013045